W9-CCT-191

Ancient ROME

Peter Connolly

OXFORD

Ancient
ROME

Peter Connolly

text by Andrew Solway

OXFORD

UNIVERSITY PRESS

OXFORD
UNIVERSITY PRESS

Great Clarendon Street, Oxford OX2 6DP

Oxford University Press is a department of the University of Oxford.
It furthers the University's objective of excellence in research, scholarship,
and education by publishing worldwide in

Oxford New York

Athens Auckland Bangkok Bogotá Buenos Aires Calcutta
Cape Town Chennai Dar es Salaam Delhi Florence Hong Kong Istanbul
Karachi Kuala Lumpur Madrid Melbourne Mexico City Mumbai
Nairobi Paris São Paulo Shanghai Singapore Taipei Tokyo Toronto Warsaw

with associated companies in Berlin Ibadan

Oxford is a registered trade mark of Oxford University Press
in the UK and in certain other countries

Text copyright © Oxford University Press 2001
Illustrations copyright © Peter Connolly 2001

The moral rights of the author/artist have been asserted

Database right Oxford University Press (maker)

First published 2001

British Library Cataloguing in Publication Data available

Hardback ISBN 0-19-910809-9

1 3 5 7 9 10 8 6 4 2

Printed in Hong Kong

Contents

The Roman empire

The Roman empire lasted for over 700 years. Rome began in about 753 BC as a small town in central Italy, on the banks of the River Tiber. At the height of the empire, the Romans ruled much of Europe and parts of Africa and Asia.

Rome was originally ruled by kings, but around 500 BC the last king was overthrown, and Rome became a republic. It was ruled by two consuls, who were elected each year, and advised by a group of elders called the Senate. The Roman republic lasted almost 500 years. But then as the empire grew, fights within the Senate led to a breakdown of the system, and single rule was brought back.

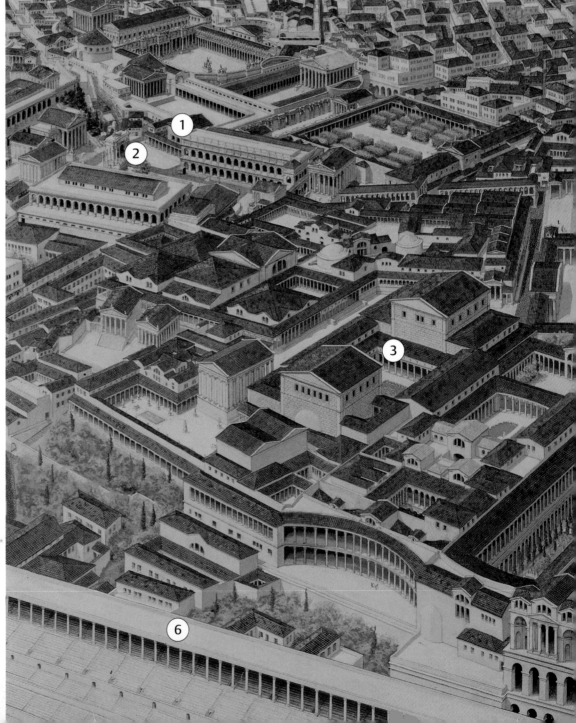

▶ The centre of Rome as it might have looked around the time of the emperor Septimius Severus (AD 193–211). The Curia (1), where the Senate met, was one of the buildings around the main square, the Forum Romanum (2). The emperor's palace (3) was close by. One of the largest buildings in Rome was the Colosseum (4). On the hill behind it are the Baths of Trajan (5). In the foreground is the race track, the Circus Maximus (6).

▼ The site of Rome.

Rome

The general Julius Caesar fought a war with a rival general, Pompey. Caesar won and became dictator, but he was murdered. Another civil war began, between Caesar's nephew Octavian and the general Mark Antony. The winner this time was Octavian. He became the first emperor of Rome, and in 27 BC he was given the name Augustus. He was the first of a line of emperors that ruled until AD 476.

The influence of Roman civilization is still around us today. Public buildings in the Roman style were built until the 19th century, and the laws of many modern countries are based on the Roman system. English, and many other European languages, are full of words from Latin, the language spoken in ancient Rome. And many modern roads follow routes that were originally Roman roads.

At home

There were more people in well-to-do Roman households than there usually are in homes today. First, there was the family itself. Then there were the household slaves, who were thought of as part of the family. Slaves who had earned their freedom could also be part of the household.

A new child

There were several ceremonies associated with a new birth. When the baby arrived the father lifted it up in his arms, to acknowledge that it was his. The baby was named when it was eight or nine days old. Boys were given two or sometimes three names. Girls in early Rome had only one name, but in later times were given two. The second name was always the family name.

▼ Roman children did not have bicycles, but they had other toys that must have been just as much fun. The boy in this carving is riding in a toy chariot pulled by a goat.

▲ This battered rag doll is nearly 2000 years old. It was found in Egypt at the time of the Roman empire.

8

◄ This carving shows a Roman school scene. Schools often held their lessons in public areas. Children had to learn their lessons off by heart, then recite them to the teacher.

▼ A child's inkwell and pens.

Toys and games

Whether they were rich or poor, Roman babies often died from diseases. This was because there were no vaccines against diseases, and no drugs to fight infections. Children that survived their early years played with toys and games, just like children today. Rag dolls have been found from Roman times, and so have spinning tops. We know that children also played board games with dice and counters.

▼ This stone board and counters were used for a board game.

Education

Not all Roman children went to school. The poorest people could not afford it, while the richest families had private tutors to teach the children at home. Boys were much more likely to go to school than girls. At primary school, children from 7 to 14 learned to read, write and do arithmetic. Some children then went on to grammar school, where they learned Greek and Latin grammar. Only the sons of rich families went on to the highest level of education – rhetoric. Rhetoric is the art of speaking well in public. It was an important skill for Romans who were likely to become lawyers, politicians, army commanders or administrators.

◄ Roman children also played with marbles.

9

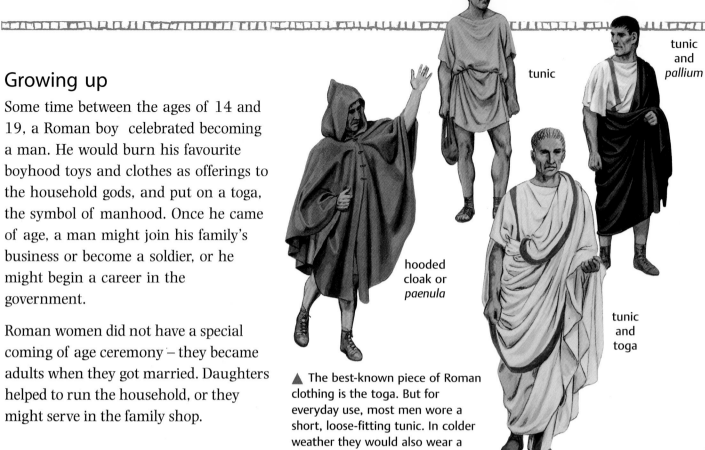

Growing up

Some time between the ages of 14 and 19, a Roman boy celebrated becoming a man. He would burn his favourite boyhood toys and clothes as offerings to the household gods, and put on a toga, the symbol of manhood. Once he came of age, a man might join his family's business or become a soldier, or he might begin a career in the government.

Roman women did not have a special coming of age ceremony – they became adults when they got married. Daughters helped to run the household, or they might serve in the family shop.

tunic

tunic and *pallium*

hooded cloak or *paenula*

tunic and toga

▲ The best-known piece of Roman clothing is the toga. But for everyday use, most men wore a short, loose-fitting tunic. In colder weather they would also wear a woollen cloak called a *pallium*.

Men and women

In Roman society, women spent most of their time at home. They did go out to shop or to visit friends, to worship at the temple or to go to the baths. But they could not take important jobs. In contrast, Roman men spent much of their daily lives away from home. Once he had finished work, a man might spend several hours at the baths, meeting with friends as well as exercising and bathing. Later, he might go to a bar to play dice, or he might get an invitation to dinner.

▶ This unusual mosaic from late Roman times shows women in bikinis. The women were probably entertainers.

Marriage

All Roman men and women were expected to get married. June was the favourite time of year for weddings.

The day before her wedding, a bride gave her childhood toys and clothes to the household gods. Early the next morning she dressed in her wedding clothes, ready for the arrival of her husband-to-be and his family and friends. The wedding ceremony took place at the bride's house, after which there was a sacrifice to the gods, and the signing of the marriage contract. Now it was time to celebrate, with a feast and dancing, After the feast, all the wedding guests joined a procession to the couple's new home.

▲ This carving shows a wedding ceremony. On the left is the bride in her wedding clothes: her *palla* would have been yellow and her veil orange. In the centre is the matron of honour, who signified harmony. The couple have linked hands as a symbol of their marriage agreement.

▼ Women wore a longer version of the men's tunic, and a version of the men's cloak called a *palla*. They did not usually wear togas. The *palla* was usually draped over the shoulder and under the right arm, with the remainder carried over the left arm.

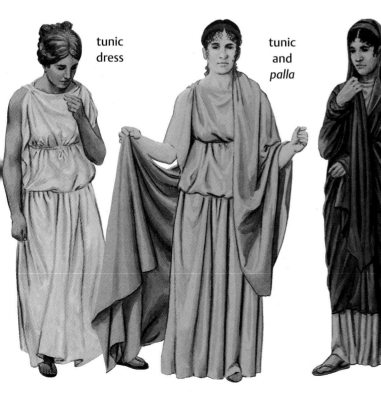

tunic dress

tunic and *palla*

palla pulled over head

▼ At the start of the empire, women's hairstyles were simple (left). Later, they became much more elaborate (right), with coiled braids and masses of curls.

Slavery

All the worst jobs in Rome were done by slaves. These were often people captured in war, who were bought and sold at market, like objects. Slaves did all the work in a Roman home. They did the cooking, the cleaning, the shopping and the laundry, and looked after the younger children. Richer households also had slaves with special skills, such as musicians and tutors.

Freedom

Slavery was not necessarily for life. Slaves could earn money and buy their freedom, or they might be freed for good service over many years, or for doing some exceptional service for their master. Freed slaves often became shopkeepers or craftsmen. They could not become full Roman citizens, but their children could.

◀ At the centre of every Roman house was a shrine to the household gods. These included the *lares*, who guarded the house against evil spirits and thieves. Every morning the head of the household would offer prayers and gifts to the *lares* and to other favourite gods.

▲ This wealthy woman is being dressed and having her hair prepared by her slave.

Death

In general, Romans did not live as long as people do today. Rich Romans had to do little work, and could expect to live to 50 or 60, but poorer people rarely lived beyond 50. When someone died, their body was displayed for several days so that friends and family could pay their respects. At the end of this time there was a funeral procession.

It was important in Roman society to be remembered after your death. So those who could afford it built elaborate tombs, designed to impress the living. Some Romans cremated (burned) their dead, then put the ashes in the tomb in a small vase or urn. Other Romans were buried without being cremated first.

▼ The remains of a Roman family tomb at Ostia. Each arched niche in the wall would have held an urn containing the ashes of a dead person.

Houses

The people of ancient Rome lived in a variety of houses and flats. The homes of the rich were often very luxurious, with cool, spacious rooms, fine furniture and shady gardens. But most Romans lived in cramped and crowded flats, or in rooms next to their shops or workshops.

Houses for the rich

Rich people's houses were usually only one or two storeys high. At the centre of the house was a court, the *atrium*. The owner of the house conducted business here each morning. The *atrium* let light into the house, and helped to keep it cool. It was covered by a roof with a hole in the middle. Rain drained through this hole into a pool below, and was stored in a cistern (tank) under the *atrium*.

▶ Some house owners built extra rooms on to their house and rented them out, or converted part of their house into flats. This picture shows a house at Herculaneum, near Pompeii. Rooms have been added at the front of the house, and jut out over the street.

14

▲ This cutaway of a Roman house shows the kitchen (1), to the left of the entrance corridor, and the dining room (2) at the back. The office opens into a small, walled garden (3).

▶ Plan of a typical Roman house.

A *atrium*
B bedroom
D dining room
G garden
S shop

The bedrooms were usually on the ground floor, and opened on to the *atrium*. Other rooms, which could be used for dining or for receiving visitors, also opened on to the *atrium*. At the back of the house was a garden. This was partly shaded by a low roof, supported by columns. Members of the household could sit out here in the cool of a summer evening. The garden might also have a fountain and an open-air dining area.

The slaves of a Roman family often had no space of their own: they had to sleep wherever they could. But some slaves had small rooms in the basement.

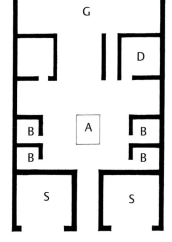

▶ This mosaic in the entrance of a house shows a chained dog with teeth bared. Underneath it says *cave canem* – 'beware of the dog'.

15

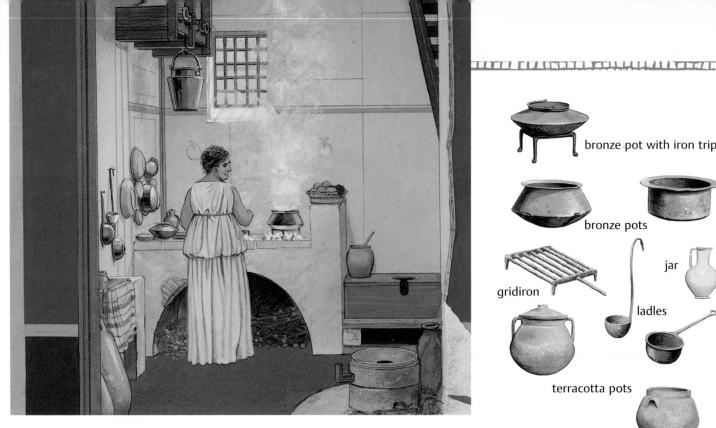

Cooking and dining

The Romans loved fine food. A good cook was a valued member of the household, even though most cooks were slaves. But the kitchen itself consisted of little more than an open counter and a sink. The counter had an arched area underneath used for storing fuel. The cook would light small fires on the counter, and either boil the food in a pot, grill it on a gridiron, or cook it under a domed cover.

Meals were an important event. The main meal was eaten in the late afternoon, and was usually three courses. The Romans liked to eat meat and drink plenty of wine. Slaves not only cooked the food, but did all the serving and clearing away as well.

▲ A Roman kitchen with cooking fires, a wood storage area and cooking implements – pots, pans, a ladle and a strainer hanging on the walls.

▼ A Roman dinner party. Wealthy Romans lay on couches to eat, and men and women ate together. Three couches were arranged around a small table. The fourth side was left open for serving.

bronze pot with iron tripod

bronze pots

gridiron

jar

ladles

terracotta pots

▲ A selection of cooking implements.

◀ Rooms were often divided by wooden partitions. Lattice-work screens were also popular, like this folding screen from Herculaneum.

▲ Wealthy Romans liked to decorate the walls and ceilings of their houses with patterns, pictures and delicate carvings. This amazing ceiling decoration comes from a bedroom in the house of the emperor Augustus.

▼ A marble table from Pompeii, elaborately carved with four lions. It probably stood in the *atrium*.

▼ Two sleeping couches with leather backs from Herculaneum.

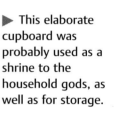

▲ This wooden bed is held together with brass fittings.

▶ This elaborate cupboard was probably used as a shrine to the household gods, as well as for storage.

◀ This bedroom has an alcove for the bed and a walk-in wardrobe.

Bedrooms

The family bedrooms opened off the *atrium*. Any windows looked into the *atrium*, rather than outside. The walls were often decorated with patterns and pictures, but there was less furniture than we are used to today. Some bedrooms had built-in wardrobes, screened off with curtains. And we know from wall paintings that Roman bedding was often striped.

▼ Most Romans had toilets in their houses. These were usually in the kitchen, because they used the same drain as the sink and could be flushed with waste water from the kitchen.

Plumbing

Rome had a regular supply of water, and an efficient drainage system. Water pipes brought supplies directly from aqueducts into private houses. And a main drain or sewer ran under most streets. But few houses were attached to this sewer. Instead, waste was collected in cesspits. It was the house owner's responsibility to make sure that these were emptied.

▼ A main drain running under the street. Lead pipes carried supplies of fresh water to houses.

Apartment blocks

Most Romans did not live in houses, but had rooms in an apartment block. Life in these blocks could be uncomfortable, even dangerous. They were often badly built, and caught fire easily, or even collapsed. There was no water supply above the first floor, and toilets were communal.

◀ Wealthy estate owners enjoyed the comforts of Roman country life. Villas like this one had mosaic floors, underfloor heating and a private bathhouse.

Country estates

Rome was surrounded by spacious estates and villas. Most of these estates were farms, and helped to supply the growing city with food, such as wheat, fruit, vegetables, olive oil, wine and meat. Almost all the work on the estate was done by slaves.

▼ This apartment block has shops on the ground floor, opening onto the street. Behind the shops are quite spacious apartments. Above are smaller flats and rooms. This block was at least three storeys high.

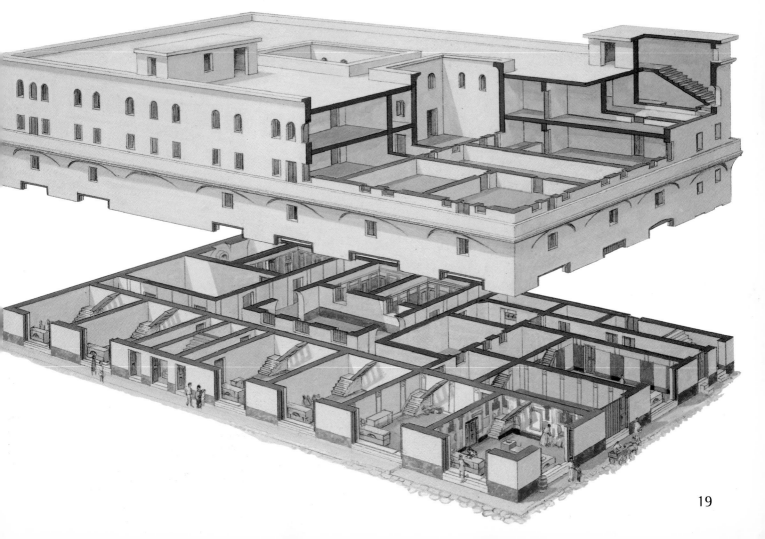

On the streets

Rome was far bigger than any other city in the ancient world. By the time of Augustus over a million people lived there. Many streets were narrow, crowded, noisy and dirty. The buildings that lined them were often dangerously tall and poorly built. It was a major problem for Rome's leaders to provide food and water for everyone living in the city.

▼ Many streets in Rome were so narrow that balconies often almost met across the street. Owners built apartment buildings higher and higher, to fit in more people. Laws restricting the height of buildings were ignored.

Street life

Walking through the Roman streets was a dangerous business. Most streets were narrow – only a few were wide enough to allow two carts to pass. Crowds of people jostled and pushed each other, and the streets were full of rubbish and sewage. It was quite common for someone in the street to be hit by rubbish tipped from an upper floor window. And many people were killed or injured in traffic accidents.

New laws

When Julius Caesar became dictator, the streets were so bad that he passed laws to try and improve things. He banned all wheeled vehicles from the street during the day, and he ordered the city's magistrates to employ people to clear up the streets. Even with the new laws, Roman streets were crowded and dirty by day. By night the streets were full of robbers and huge carts. No-one went out without an armed guard.

▶ Carts were used to transport all kinds of goods into Rome from the surrounding countryside and from Portus, Rome's sea port.

▲ This cobbled street in the centre of Rome dates from Roman times.

Police and firefighters

Rome's streets would have been even more dangerous without the three urban cohorts. These were the Roman equivalent of a police force. They were set up by the emperor Augustus to fight crime in the city. Each cohort had 1500 soldiers, who served for 20 years. Augustus also set up a force of 7000 night police, called the *vigiles*. As well as fighting crime, the *vigiles* were the city's fire brigade.

Food from abroad

As Rome grew in size, it became difficult to supply the city with food from the surrounding countryside. Gradually more and more food was brought by ship from other parts of the empire. Wine came from Gaul (modern France) and Spain, and olive oil from southern Spain and north Africa. But the most important food that came from abroad was wheat. This came from Egypt in huge grain ships, some of which may have carried over 1000 tonnes.

▶ This picture shows Roman freighter ships, similar to the ships that carried grain from Egypt to Rome, at the port of Classis, near Ravenna. Classis was the Roman word for a fleet, and Classis was the main Roman naval base in northern Italy.

▲ Large pottery jars like this were called amphorae. Romans used them for transporting all kinds of goods, from wine and olive oil to dried fruit.

Bread for the poor

From the early days of the republic, there were often shortages of food. To try and help the situation, from about 75 BC the city's rulers gave out free grain to the poorer citizens. In later times (after AD 270) the grain was ground and made into bread before being handed out. By then over 200,000 people were being given free food.

▲ Bakers ground the flour as well as baking bread. The donkey is turning a mill, which the grinds the grain between two heavy stones.

Water on pipe

Much of Rome's water came from aqueducts. These were channels that brought water from springs east of Rome, into the city. Once the water reached the city, it travelled through smaller pipes to public fountains in the streets, to the public baths, and to a few individual houses.

Waste water from the baths and streets went through a system of underground drains to the river Tiber. Most private houses were not connected to this main drainage system. Instead, people often threw their waste into the streets, or they took it to a nearby cesspit.

◀ Aqueducts had to keep an almost level course, even when crossing a valley. Roman engineers built strong, arched structures to carry the water.

Shopping

Ancient Rome was a great place for shopping. In the Forum Boarium, you could buy all kinds of meat, while the Forum Holitorium was the place to buy fruit and vegetables. If you wanted fish for dinner, you could choose it live from a tank. And there were all kinds of other shops lining Rome's main streets – shops for shoes, knives, rope, pottery, wine, bread and many other things. Poorer women did all their own shopping, but in wealthier households the shopping was done by slaves.

▼ Shops in a Roman street.

Showing the wares

Most shops were simply a single room with a wooden or stone counter for displaying goods. To advertise themselves, shops usually had a sign outside – 'Shoe Repairs' or 'Books'. Glass was too expensive for shops to have big windows, so they were usually open to the street. At night, shop owners put up wooden shutters to keep out thieves. Any thieves that did get into a shop at night would have to be very quiet, because most shopkeepers and their families lived in a small flat above the shop.

▶ A small Roman weighing scale. Standard weights and measures were used throughout the Roman empire. Inspectors visited shops regularly to make sure they were using the correct measures.

▲ Roman money. The gold *aureus* (bottom) was worth 25 silver *denarii* (centre), or 100 *sestertii* (top). A Roman citizen had to earn over 400,000 *sestertii* per year to become a knight, the middle rank of citizen.

▲ Trajan's Markets were the Roman equivalent of a shopping mall. There were over 150 separate shops and offices. One group of shops curved around a semicircular street. There was also a large arched hall with shops on two levels.

Work

Rome and its vast empire needed all kinds of workers to keep it going. The Roman army needed thousands of soldiers. The senators and other politicians needed civil servants to keep things running smoothly. Rome needed farmers to grow food, craftsmen to make things, and merchants to sell them. And it needed slaves to do all the dirty, difficult or dangerous work.

◀ Slaves did all the really heavy work in Rome. This statuette shows an actor playing the part of a slave.

▶ Roman soldiers carried a short sword, a shield and a heavy javelin (throwing spear). They wore iron plate armour on their upper body. The helmet had an extension at the back to protect the neck, and hinged cheek pieces.

Soldiers

The Roman soldier, or legionary, was the backbone of the army. A legionary was expected to march all day, carrying all his own equipment, dig an earthwork for a temporary camp, and still be ready to fight the next morning.

In early Roman times, every Roman citizen who could afford the equipment had to serve in the army part of the time. But soon the empire grew too big for this system to work, and soldiers became full-time professionals. Many poorer men became soldiers because they could earn more money than in civilian life. And men from other parts of the empire joined up because if they survived 25 years in the army they were given Roman citizenship.

Senators and 'civil servants'

Only men from Rome's noble families could become senators (the most important politicians). Politicians were not paid, and so only the rich could afford to go into politics. Many more people were part of the Roman 'civil service', the administrators who looked after the day-to-day affairs of the empire. Civil servants did everything from supervising the building of a new port to organizing groups of slaves to clean the streets.

Merchants and craftsmen

Middle-ranking Romans were often businessmen. They made their money buying and selling everything from basic foods to jewellery and perfume. Transport was expensive, so only luxuries could be imported from other countries.

Everyday items were all made locally by craftsmen in workshops. Some craftsmen owned or rented their own workshops and sold their goods directly to customers. Others were part of larger workshops run by businessmen. There were craftsmen making simple items in all kinds of materials – carpenters, stone masons, tile and brick makers, bronze workers and blacksmiths, rope makers and glass-blowers. There were also more skilled craftsmen such as goldsmiths, jewellers and mosaic makers. Many goldsmiths and jewellers were based near the Forum Romanum.

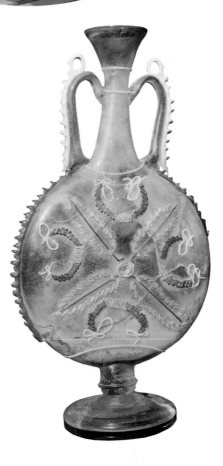

▲ Often a craftsman's workshop was also a shop. In this bronzesmith's workshop, the smith himself is at work in the back, while his wife sells the things he has made at the front.

▶ This beautiful glass bottle was probably used by a Roman woman for storing perfumed oil. From the time of Augustus onwards, glassware was popular in Rome.

The theatre

In early Rome, permanent theatres were banned. Temporary theatres were built for a particular festival, then taken down afterwards. Most of these structures were wooden, but some hardly sound temporary at all. The writer Pliny described a theatre built for a festival in 58 BC. The back of the stage rose up in three storeys: the lowest had columns of marble, the next columns of glass, and the topmost columns of gilded wood!

The Theatre of Pompey

The first permanent theatre in Rome was built by the Roman general Pompey in 55 BC. It seated about 27,000 people. The seating area was similar to that of a Greek theatre – a series of semicircular steps rising up in tiers from ground level. The Temple of Venus Victrix was built at the top of the seating area.

◀ One of the arches of the Theatre of Marcellus as it looks today.

posts for awning

seating area

arched corridors

The Theatre of Marcellus

Another, smaller theatre, the Theatre of Marcellus, was built by the emperor Augustus in 13 or 11 BC. We know quite a lot about this theatre because the building is still standing. It held about 14,000 people. The seating area was supported by three levels of arched vaults. Both the Theatre of Pompey and the Theatre of Marcellus had elaborate stage buildings, which formed a backdrop to the action on stage. These were two or three storeys high, with columns on each level.

stage building

◀ A cutaway showing the arched corridors that support the seating of the Theatre of Marcellus. The seating area is still there today, but the stage building has been destroyed.

▼ This is how the Theatre of Pompey may have looked. The awning, designed to shade spectators from the sun, may not have covered the whole seating area. The building at the back of the seating area is the Temple of Venus Victrix.

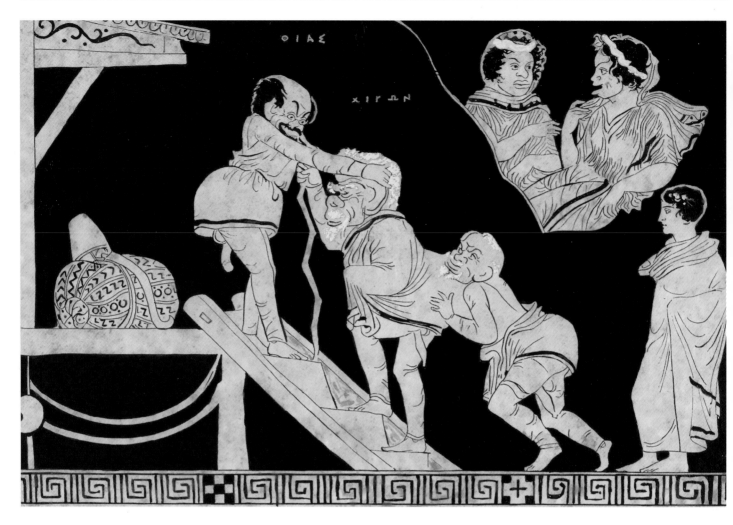

Tragedy and comedy

Roman plays were often based on the tragedies and comedies of Ancient Greece. Playwrights such as the tragedy writer Seneca, and the comedy writers Plautus and Terence, wrote plays to be performed at religious festivals. But Romans also liked a more slapstick kind of humour. In some plays, actors wore exaggerated masks and padded their clothes to give themselves enormous stomachs and bottoms. There were also farces involving characters that the audience would recognize: Bucco and Maccus the fools, Dosenus and Manducus the greedy pigs, and Pappus, the boss.

▲ This southern Italian vase painting shows the kind of comic play that early Roman comedies were based on. Two servants help an old man on to the stage. All three are wearing masks and padding. The actor on the right, with no mask or padding, is playing the hero, Achilles.

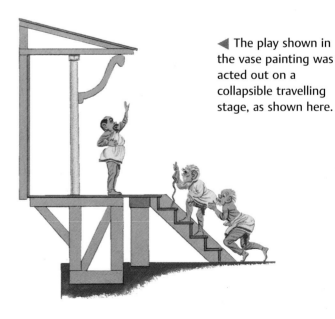

◄ The play shown in the vase painting was acted out on a collapsible travelling stage, as shown here.

Mime and pantomime

By the first century BC, comedies and tragedies in the Greek style were no longer popular. Now people wanted to see mime and pantomime.

Mime shows were not plays without words. They were adventure tales, sometimes very rude, with songs and music. Pantomime was more like what we would call mime today. Here, a single actor called the *pantomimus* ('one who imitates all things') acted out the main story of the play. He was supported by music and masked dancers miming the actions.

Actors

Actors were often slaves or freedmen, because acting was not thought to be a very respectable profession. But a good *pantomimus* could become a household name, just like a film star today. An actor, especially a *pantomimus,* had to play several different parts within a show. So he would wear masks to help distinguish the different characters.

▲ Two statuettes of actors. The bronze statuette (left) shows a comic actor. The marble statuette (right) shows a tragic actor.

▼ A selection of actors' masks. The characters are (from left) a tragic hero, a tragic heroine, a comic old man, a comic young man and a comic slave.

At the races

The Romans loved watching sports. Games and races were a regular part of life in the city. And the most popular events of all were the chariot races. These included two-, three- and four-horse races, and were held in Rome's main stadium, the Circus Maximus. Thousands came to watch.

▲ One of the twelve starting gates. At the signal to start, an attendant pulled a lever which operated a catapult system, jerking out the latches of the gates so that they all flew open at once.

Chariots, horses and drivers

Chariot racing was a very serious business. Large stables supplied the horses, chariots and drivers. Lots of people worked in these stables: coaches, trainers, blacksmiths, vets and grooms. The charioteers themselves belonged to one of four teams, and each team had its own colour: white, red, blue or green.

▼ The charioteers had to turn as tightly as possible round the turning posts (*metae*) – the three large cones on the right. The seven eggs at the centre marked the seven laps of the race. As each lap was completed, one egg was removed.

The races

On a race day, the public crowded into the stadium. Many people placed bets. A magistrate signalled the start of a race by dropping a cloth. The chariots entered through individual starting gates (*carceres*). They raced anti-clockwise, and had to circle the *spina* – a platform running down the centre of the stadium – seven times. Crashes were common.

There could be 24 races in a full day's programme. Most were two- or four-horse chariot races, but there were novelty races as well. Teams of up to six horses might be used, or the chariots might be pulled by elephants or camels. At the end of the games the victors received prizes – the victor's palm, crowns and gold necklaces.

The stadium

The Circus Maximus was the biggest and most important stadium in Rome. It was originally laid out in the 6th century BC, and for many centuries it was made of wood. But the emperors Titus and Trajan had the whole thing rebuilt in concrete, brick and stone around the end of the 1st century AD. They also made it bigger. The improved Circus Maximus was 570 metres long, 140 metres wide and could seat an incredible 250,000 people.

▼ The Circus Maximus.

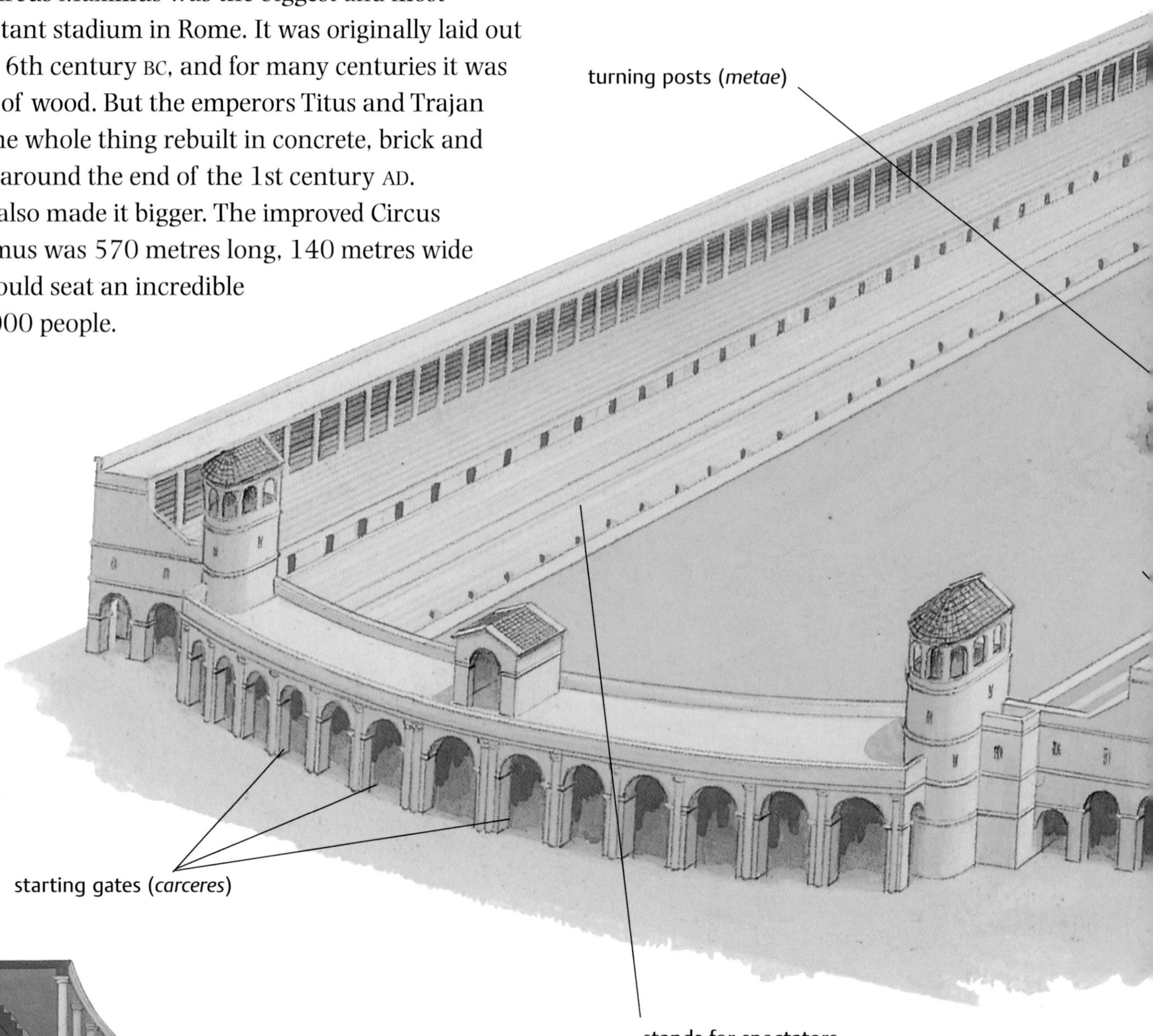

turning posts (*metae*)

starting gates (*carceres*)

stands for spectators

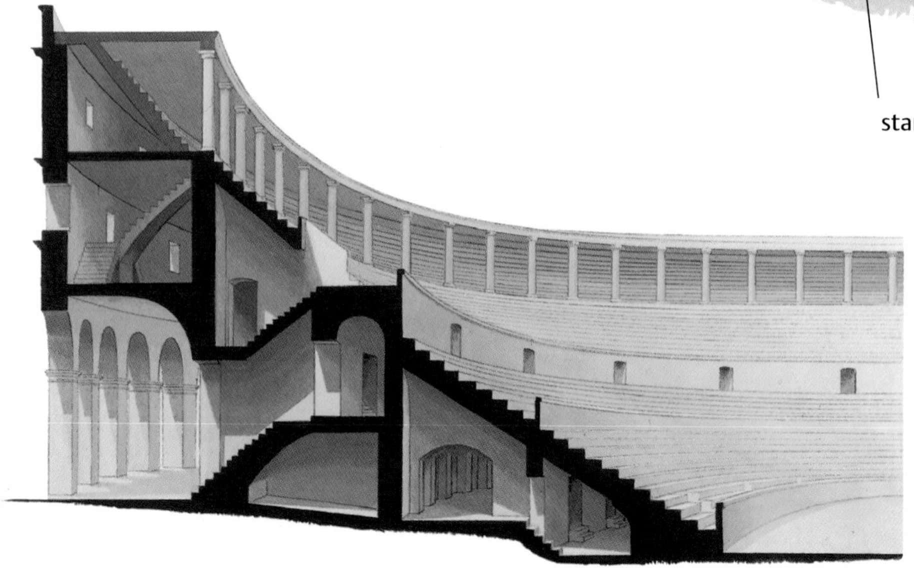

◀ A cross-section through the stands of the Circus Maximus, to show how they were built. Only the galleries at the top were shaded from the sun.

Titus's triumphal arch

imperial box (*pulvinar*)

spina, decorated with trophies and statues

The stands

The stands were about 28 metres high. They were made of concrete, brick and stone. The seating was supported by three rows of high arches and inside these a network of passageways and staircases brought the spectators to their seats. An arcade ran round the outside of the stadium. The Circus was set in a valley, not on its own as shown here.

racing track

▶ Most charioteers were slaves, but those who were successful could buy their freedom with their prize money. Champion charioteers were idolized by the public, and some became very rich and famous.

The amphitheatre

A Roman amphitheatre was as big as a modern football stadium. But Romans did not go there to watch football. The amphitheatre was the setting for gladiatorial games – contests between professional fighters that were often fought to the death.

▼ This cutaway shows the Colosseum arena and the maze of tunnels, corridors and ramps beneath it. The posts around the top of the seating area supported an awning that could be put up to protect spectators from the sun.

Wooden amphitheatres

The first gladiatorial contest, in 264 BC, involved just three pairs of gladiators. But by the time of Julius Caesar 200 years later, gladiatorial games were huge events, with hundreds of gladiatorial contests and wild animal fights. Like the theatres, early amphitheatres were temporary wooden structures. A stone amphitheatre was built in 29 BC, but it was destroyed in AD 64. To replace it, the emperors Vespasian and Titus built the amphitheatre we call the Colosseum.

support for awning

entrances and exits

emperor's box

trapdoors

senator's seat

The Colosseum

The Colosseum was completed in AD 80. It was enormous – 188 metres long, 156 metres wide and 40 metres high. It could seat over 50,000 people. The five tiers of seating around the central arena were reached from 76 entrances at ground level. Under the floor of the arena there was a complicated system of lifts, and ramps leading to trapdoors in the arena floor. Wild animals could be released through these trapdoors. There was also a tunnel to the Ludus Magnus, where the gladiators lived and trained.

▲ The outside of the Colosseum as it looks today.

▼ On the south side of the Colosseum there was a ceremonial entrance for the emperor. A similar entrance on the north side was for magistrates. These were magnificently decorated.

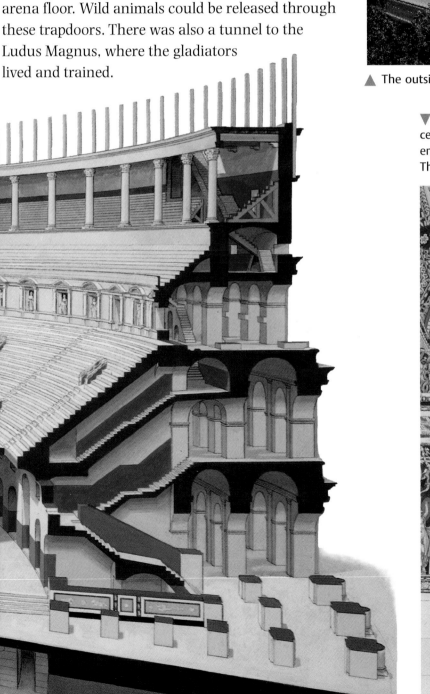

Gladiators

The first gladiators were prisoners of war and slaves. But by the time of the Roman emperors, gladiators included freedmen, professional fighters and some women. We know the names of about 20 different types of gladiator, but we do not know how most of them were armed, or how they fought. The best known gladiators are the heavily armed Samnite, or *hoplomachus*, and the lightly armed *retiarius*, who fought with a net and trident. A third type, the *secutor*, had an egg-shaped helmet. This was specially designed so that it would not catch in the net of his main opponent, the *retiarius*.

◄ ► A statuette of a *hoplomachus*, and *hoplomachus* helmet and greaves (leg-guards) found in Pompeii.

Training gladiators

Before they fought in the arena, gladiators had to be trained at a *ludus*, or training school. Gladiators ate well, and their living quarters were comfortable. But they had to work extremely hard, and discipline was very strict. Every group of gladiators had to swear an oath to their *lanista*, or trainer, ' ... to obey in everything. To endure imprisonment, flogging and even death by the sword.' Training a good gladiator took years, so very few contests were actually fought to the death. It was possible for a gladiator to grow rich and famous.

◄ ▼ A statuette of a *secutor,* and a *secutor* helmet found in Pompeii.

Spartacus

Spartacus is one of the few gladiators whose name is known today. He was a slave who trained at the best *ludus*, in Capua. In 73 BC he began what became the biggest slave revolt in the history of the Roman empire. He gathered a huge band of followers, and for two years they defeated all the Roman troops sent against them. His army was eventually defeated by the general Crassus in 71 BC. Spartacus and many of his followers were put to death.

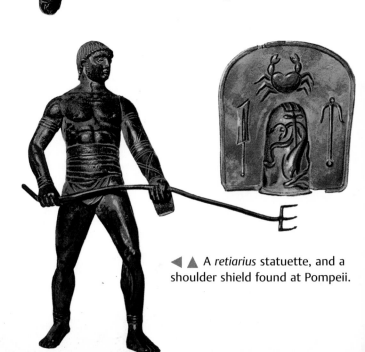

◄ ▲ A *retiarius* statuette, and a shoulder shield found at Pompeii.

▼ A reconstruction of the Ludus Magnus, the main gladiator training school in Rome. In the background is the Colosseum.

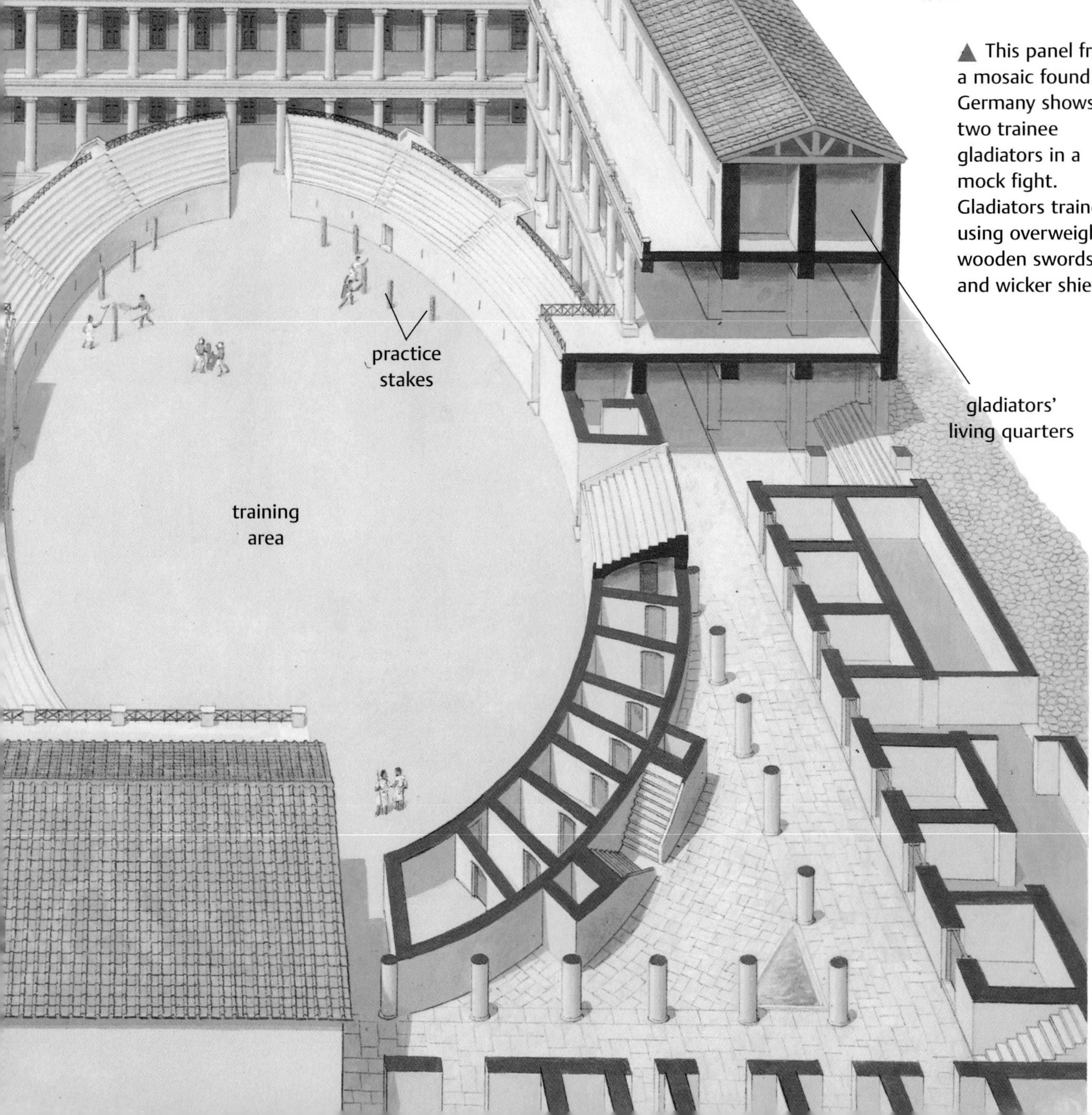

▲ This panel from a mosaic found in Germany shows two trainee gladiators in a mock fight. Gladiators trained using overweight wooden swords and wicker shields.

practice stakes

gladiators' living quarters

training area

The opening procession

The Colosseum was ready to open in the summer of AD 80, and an inccredible celebration was arranged. There was a festival of gladiatorial games that went on for 100 days. The show began with a grand procession of gladiators, marching into the Colosseum two by two carrying their shields and weapons. The procession was played into the arena by trumpeters.

Wild beast shows

In the morning the games began with wild animal displays. Pairs of wild animals fought each other, and hunters fought with wild animals using a variety of weapons. By the time the Colosseum opened, all kinds of animals were used in the games. There were big cats such as lions and leopards, elephants, crocodiles, rhinoceroses, hippopotamuses – even ostriches.

▲ These two mosaics show hunters, or *venatores*. Each has a whip in his right hand, while the left arm is padded to protect it from bites.

◀ This stone carving on a Roman tomb shows the gladiatorial procession at the start of the games. The gladiators are shown carrying their helmets; behind them is a trumpeter.

The gladiators fight

In the afternoons, the gladiators fought. Several contests would happen in the arena at the same time, each with its own referee. Usually two different types of gladiator would fight, for example a *secutor* versus a *retiarius*. If one of the gladiators was seriously injured, the referee would stop the fight, and the wounded man would appeal for mercy. If he had fought well, he would be spared.

◀ A contest between a *secutor* and a *retiarius*. The *retiarius* is wounded and has lost his net. The official wearing black in the background may be called in if the losing gladiator gets the 'thumbs down'. He will have to put the loser to death.

41

The baths

Romans liked to keep clean. They liked to bathe at least once a day. But most people did not have individual baths in their houses. Instead, they went to large public baths, where they could relax, meet friends and exercise as well as bathe.

▼ The Stabian baths at Pompeii. There were separate baths for men and women. You can see the changing rooms (1), the warm rooms (2), the hot rooms (3), the cold rooms (4), the exercise yard (5) and the swimming pool (6).

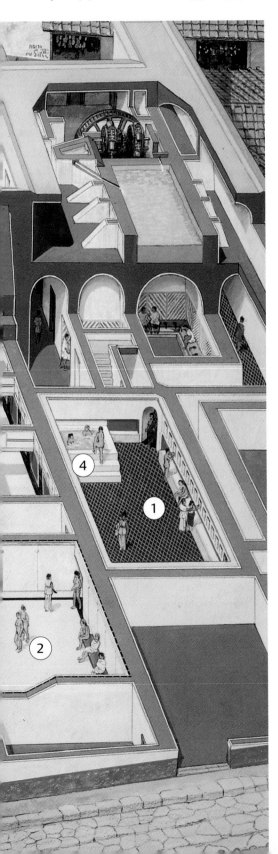

◀ The hot room in the women's baths

A visit to the baths

Romans who could spare the time spent several hours at the baths each day. They left their clothes in the changing room, keeping only a towel. Then they might go out to exercise, or into the warm room, where they could sit and chat, or even do business. Once warmed up, they went into the hot room, where it was hot and steamy. Afterwards, they would finish with a refreshing plunge into a pool of cold water in the cold room.

▼ Water for the baths was heated in a tank, then piped into a basin heated by a furnace under the floor. Cooler water sank to the bottom of the bath, where it was reheated, while hotter water rose to the surface.

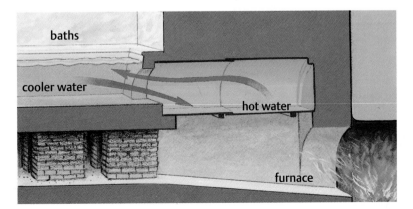

baths

cooler water

hot water

furnace

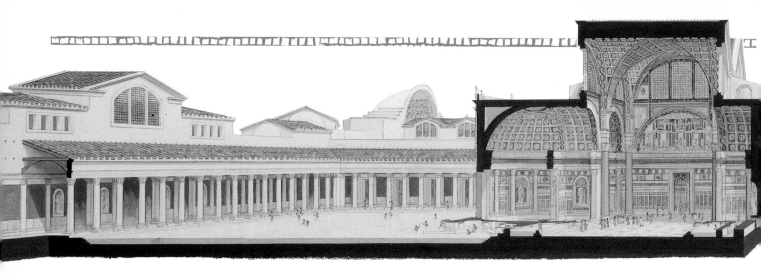

The imperial baths

By the end of the Roman empire, there were over 800 public baths in Rome. The largest and most impressive were the 11 imperial baths, each built by a different emperor. The Baths of Trajan, for example, were enormous. They were built on a huge artificial platform over 300 metres long, on the side of the Esquiline Hill. Each of the main bathing areas had a high, domed ceiling covered with beautiful decoration. There was room for hundreds of people to bathe at the same time.

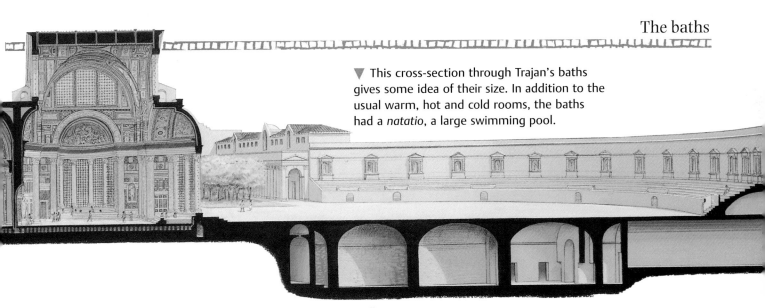

▼ This cross-section through Trajan's baths gives some idea of their size. In addition to the usual warm, hot and cold rooms, the baths had a *natatio*, a large swimming pool.

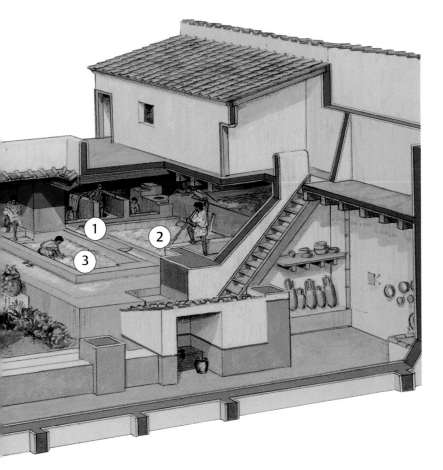

▲ This *fullonica* was converted from a large house. The three tanks on the right (1, 2 and 3) were where the clothes were washed and rinsed. Clothes were dried on racks on the roof.

The laundry

A Roman laundry was called a *fullonica*. This was because as well as being a place for washing clothes, it was also a fuller's, where woven cloth was bleached and finished. The process involved stiffening the cloth, washing out dirt and grease, stretching and beating the cloth, combing it to bring up the nap, trimming the surface, then finally pressing it.

▼ Romans did not use soap for washing. Instead, they rubbed perfumed olive oil on themselves and then scraped off the oil and dirt with a blade called a strigil. This picture shows several strigils and an oil bottle.

45

Eating out

There were lots of different places in Rome where people could eat out – or even get a take-away. They ranged from hole-in-the-wall bars serving hot food, to spacious restaurants with courtyards and fountains.

Bars and take-aways

Some Roman bars were just drinking dens, but more often they also served hot food. Poorer families living in wooden buildings often relied on these bars for hot meals, because it was against the law to light fires in wooden buildings. Some bars had places to sit, others did take-aways. Families could also get food cooked for them at bakeries, which offered a service as a 'public oven'.

Restaurants

Richer families more often ate at home, as they had kitchens, and slaves to cook their meals. But there were also restaurants for richer citizens. One at Ostia had benches outside for customers wanting a drink or a snack, and tables inside for people wanting a proper meal. Customers could choose to either sit or recline at the table.

▲ This is how the restaurant at Ostia might have looked. Romans ate many kinds of fish and meat, including dormice and small birds.

◀ A small bar found at Pompeii. The deep jars sunk into the counter may have held dried beans or grain. Upstairs there were rooms for guests.

Spices and sauces

Romans liked their food hot and spicy. They used spices and strong-flavoured sauces in all their cooking. Even sweet dishes were often flavoured with pepper. Pasta had not been invented at that time, but Romans did make *ofellae*, a kind of pizza. But there was one big difference – Romans did not have tomatoes!

▲ This cooking equipment was found at the bar in Herculaneum. It includes half a tray (1), a mortar for grinding spices (2), a quern for grinding corn to flour (3) and several cooking pots.

The Roman forum

Every Roman town had a forum – an open space that acted as a
market place or town square. The greatest of these was the Forum
Romanum in Rome. In the early days of Rome the forum was a
meeting place and a shopping centre. It was also the place where
people assembled to make decisions and vote.

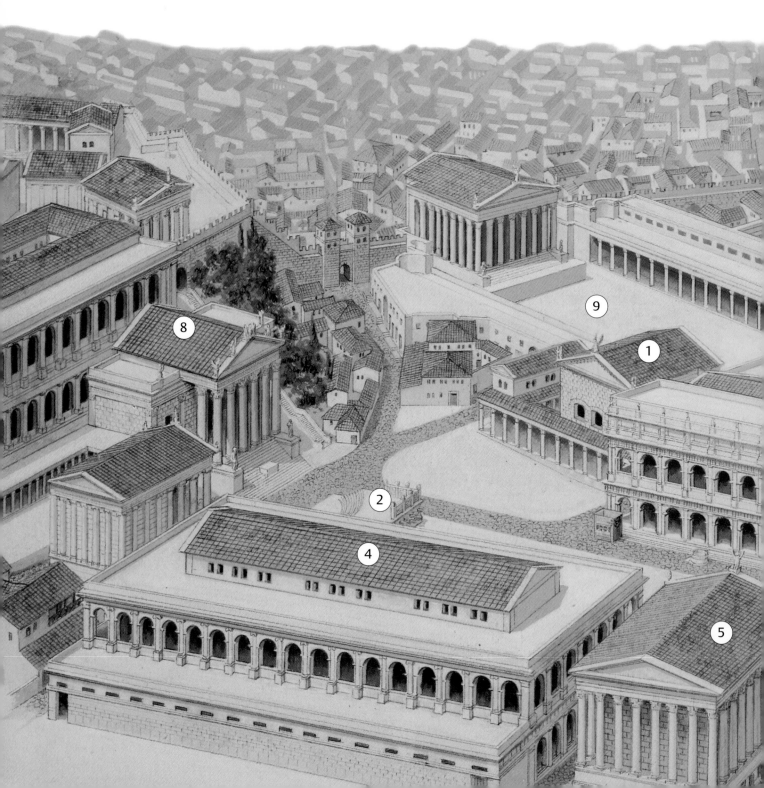

Rebuilt in marble

Some of Rome's most important and sacred buildings were built around the Forum Romanum. Several temples were built there, and also the Curia – the meeting place for the senators, Rome's most important citizens.

When Augustus became emperor in 27 BC, he began a tremendous building programme in and around the Forum Romanum. The outsides of these new buildings were covered with beautiful marble. The Forum became a showplace for the might of Rome.

◀ The Forum Romanum at the time of Augustus. Next to the Curia on the north-east side was the Basilica Paulli (a basilica was a large building where there were law courts). Opposite this were a temple and another basilica. In the centre of the forum was the Rostra – a platform from which Rome's leaders could make speeches.

1   The Curia
2   Rostra
3   Basilica Paulli
4   Basilica Julia
5   Temple of Castor and Pollux
6   Temple of Julius Caesar
7   Temple of Vesta
8   Temple of Concord
9   Forum of Julius Caesar
10 Forum of Augustus

▼ The ruins of the Forum Romanum have been excavated, and can be seen today. Parts of the Temple of Castor and Pollux (5) still stand.

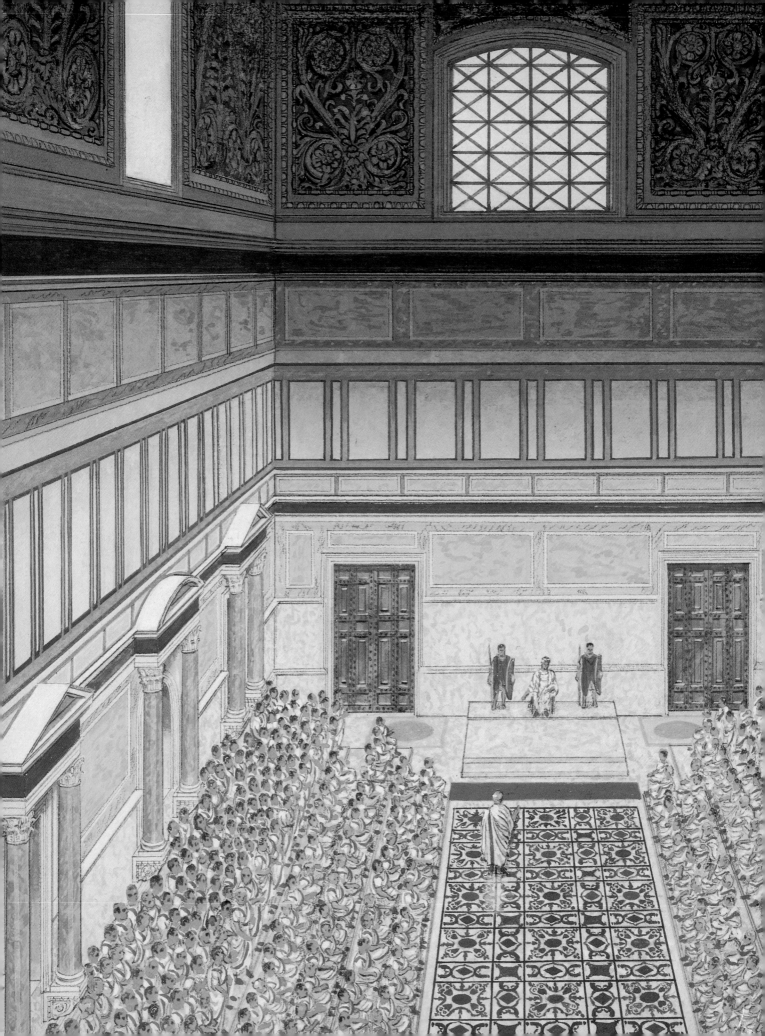

▶ The Curia as it looks today. The columned walkway that used to run across the front of the building is no longer standing.

The Senate

When Rome was a republic, it was ruled by two officials, called the consuls. The consuls were elected each year by an assembly of all Roman citizens. The consuls had many officials to help them – the praetors, who were the deputy consuls, quaestors, who looked after the government's money, and aediles, who organized all the public building projects. But most important was a group of older advisers, many of whom had been consuls themselves. These were the senators. The empire was run by the Senate and the ruling consuls.

The emperor

When Augustus first became emperor, he took over much of the Senate's power. Consuls were still elected every year – but Augustus made sure that he himself, or someone he chose, was elected. He also appointed the men who ruled Rome's most difficult provinces and many other officials.

In Augustus's time the Senate still had some power, but under later emperors they became gradually less important. To stay in power an emperor needed the support of the army, not the Senate.

◀ Inside the Curia, where the Senate met. At first there were about 300 senators, but by the time of Augustus there were nearly 1000, and there were never enough seats for everyone.

51

Other fora

Most Roman towns had only one forum, but Rome itself had many. As the Forum Romanum became more of a show place, the shops moved to other fora. Julius Caesar and Augustus built impressive new fora near the Forum Romanum. Later emperors built even more magnificent fora. The largest of all was Trajan's Forum, which the emperor Trajan built with money from his successful wars against a people in eastern Europe called the Dacians.

▼ A reconstruction of how Trajan's Forum might have looked. Across one end is the huge Basilica Ulpia, one of the largest buildings in Rome at this time. Rising above the basilica in the background is Trajan's column.

▼ Trajan built this tall marble column in his forum, to commemorate his victory against the Dacians. A spiral carving running right up the column shows scenes from the Dacian wars. Trajan's column can still be seen in modern Rome.

Trajan's column

Basilica Ulpia

Trajan's Forum

Law and order

Early in Rome's history, the Romans wrote down their most important laws and displayed them in the Forum Romanum. Buildings in the Forum Romanum and other fora were used as public courts, where someone who had broken the law could be brought before a judge. Different courts dealt with different parts of the law. For instance, the court of the *centumviri* (hundred men) dealt with disputes over who should inherit a person's wealth when they died. Roman laws survived after the empire itself collapsed. The laws of many modern countries are based on the Roman system.

Punishments depended on the class of the criminal. Poorer people and slaves suffered beatings or execution. They might even be sentenced to die in the arena, torn apart by wild beasts or impaled on stakes. Richer people were executed in private or sent into exile, or they might have their property taken away from them.

▲ Romans were not usually imprisoned for their crimes. Rich citizens were punished by loss of rank or land, while poorer people might be sent to the mines. However this prison, close to the Curia, was used for people who were going to be executed.

Trajan's Markets

Victory celebrations

Successful generals, like Trajan in his campaign against the Dacians, were celebrated when they returned to Rome. Most of Rome's immense wealth came from the riches captured during the wars, and from the taxes raised in the conquered lands. Prisoners of war were also brought to Rome, and were sold in the slave markets.

A triumph

For a truly brilliant victory, the Senate would award a public triumph. The victorious general and his army would ride through the city streets in a grand procession, displaying treasures captured during the campaign, and a long line of prisoners. Cheering crowds lined the streets for these victory processions.

▶ The Arch of Titus was built as a monument to Titus's victory. Carvings on the arch show scenes from the triumphal procession.

◀ The emperor Vespasian's son, Titus, was awarded a triumph in AD 70, for his capture of the city of Jerusalem. This picture of the procession shows treasures, captives, and bulls, which would have been sacrificed in the temples, parading through the streets.

▶ This statue from Trajan's Forum shows a Dacian leader captured during Trajan's campaign. Many statues like this decorated the forum.

Many gods

The people who first built Rome were farmers and shepherds. They worshipped gods of nature. They worshipped a god of the sky, for example, and gods of freshwater springs and forests. To be sure of a good crop or a successful lambing, they would make a sacrifice or an offering to one of the gods.

Roman and Greek gods

The most important of the Roman gods was Jupiter, the sky god. His wife Juno was the chief god for women, especially married women. The Romans also adopted several important gods from the Greeks, such as Apollo, god of healing, and Cybele, the *Magna Mater* ('Great Mother'). Jupiter and Juno's daughter Minerva was the goddess of crafts and the arts, but she was also identified with Athena, a Greek goddess of war.

All these gods had their own temples and festivals, where people could make offerings to obtain their favour.

▲ At religious festivals, and when beginning any important enterprise, Romans made sacrifices to the gods. The top picture shows the sacrifice of a boar, a ram and a bull. The bottom picture shows the emperor pouring an offering of wine on the altar.

▲ The first temple of Jupiter Optimus Maximus, on top of the Capitoline hill, was built in about 500 BC. It overlooked the Forum Romanum, the corner of which can be seen bottom right.

▶ Vestal Virgins were the only female priests in Rome. Vestals were chosen when they were young girls, and served for 30 years. During this time they were not allowed to marry.

Vesta and Roma

Two godesses that were especially important to Rome were the goddesses Roma and Vesta. Roma was the personification of Rome itself. Vesta was the goddess of the sacred eternal flame, a fire that burned in the Temple of Vesta in the Forum Romanum. People believed that while the sacred flame burned, Rome would remain strong. Six priestesses, the Vestal Virgins, had the job of tending the sacred flame.

◀ This Roman mosaic found in Tunisia shows the goddess Minerva and a river god. As well as the great gods, the Romans believed that there were lesser gods in every wood, mountain and river.

Emperors as gods

The Romans believed that each person has a god-like side to them, which they called a person's *genius*. When he became emperor, Augustus encouraged people to worship his *genius*. After he died he was made into a god. Temples were built to him, and a group of priests called the Augustales were set up. Later emperors were often worshipped as gods while they were alive.

▼ Priests making offerings outside the Temple of Isis in Pompeii. Isis was worshipped by women, and was credited with giving women more power in Roman society.

Foreign gods

As Romans conquered the countries around the eastern Mediterranean, they came into contact with many eastern religions. The worship of some of these gods was taken up in Rome. The goddess Isis, for example, had a temple in Rome, although the worship of Isis began originally in Egypt. Mithras was another eastern god who was Romanized. He was originally worshipped in Persia (modern Iran). Soldiers and traders were often followers of Mithras.

▲ Temples to Mithras were often underground chambers or caves. These two figures were often found at the entrance. The figure with the raised torch indicates the day, while the other indicates night.

▲ A statue of the emperor Augustus as a god. Augustus is shown as a general, wearing a richly decorated breastplate and an officer's cloak. His right hand may originally have held a lance.

The Pantheon

One of the great surviving masterpieces of Roman building is a temple dedicated to all the gods. The Pantheon was built between AD 118 and 125, during the time of the emperor Hadrian. The most spectacular part of the building is the main circular space, the Rotunda. The roof of the Rotunda is a vast dome over 40 metres across. No building with a larger dome was built until over 1300 years later. The Pantheon still stands in Rome today.

◀ The ceiling of the dome is divided into small squares called coffers. The whole ceiling would originally have been beautifully painted.

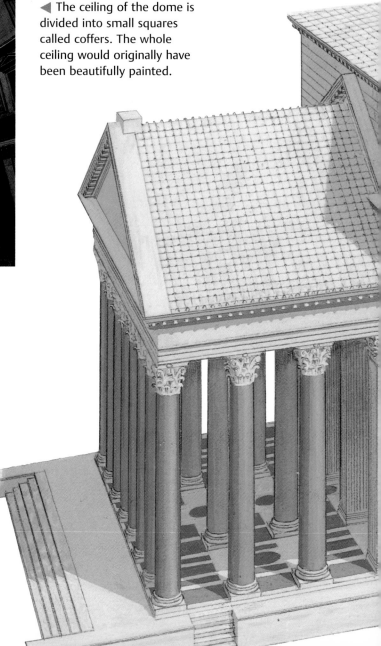

Christianity

One of the 'foreign religions' introduced into Rome was Christianity. Romans were quite tolerant of most religions, but Christians were often attacked for their beliefs. In AD 64 a great fire destroyed much of Rome, and the emperor of the time, Nero, blamed the Christians for it. For over 200 years, many of them were put to death in terrible ways. But in AD 313, during the rule of the emperor Constantine, Christianity was recognized as an official religion in Rome.

This cutaway of the Pantheon shows how the weight of the roof is supported by both an outer and an inner wall. The dome itself is very thick at the base, and gradually thins. The upper parts of the dome are made from a very light stone called tufa.

Glossary

amphitheatre: a large stadium where audiences came to watch gladiatorial games.

amphora (plural amphorae): a two-handled jar used for storing and transporting wine, olive oil and many other things.

aqueduct: an artificial channel for carrying water. Rome's water supply came via aqueducts from rivers in the surrounding countryside.

atrium: the hall or entrance area of a Roman house.

basilica: a large hall or building used for law courts or for public meetings.

Circus Maximus: a large stadium in Rome where chariot races were held.

Colosseum: the amphitheatre in Rome, where gladiatorial games were held.

consul: one of two senior magistrates, or judges, elected in Rome each year.

Curia: the meeting place for the Roman Senate.

forum (plural fora): a public square or marketplace in a Roman town.

Forum Romanum: the main forum in the centre of Rome.

gladiator: a professional fighter, who took part in gladiatorial shows.

lanista: someone who trained gladiators, and also refereed gladiatorial contests.

lares: Roman household gods, the spirits of a family's ancestors.

legionary: a Roman foot soldier.

ludus: a training school for gladiators.

numina (plural *numinae*): early Roman gods of the woods, fields and rivers.

Pantheon: a temple in Rome dedicated to all the gods.

pantomimus: a Roman actor who acted out all the parts in a play.

penates: Roman household gods, guardians of the larder.

rhetoric: the art of good public speaking.

Senate: a group of important Romans who met to make decisions about how Rome was governed.

senator: a member of the Senate.

sewer: a channel or pipe for carrying away waste water.

toga: a garment worn by Roman officials and other citizens. It consisted of a large semicircle of white cloth that was draped around the body.

Index

Acknowledgements

The publishers would like to thank the following for permission to reproduce photographs.

Page 10br The Bridgeman Art Library; 21bc, 27br Ancient Art and Architecture; 28bc Scala; 56bc, 59tr, 60tl AKG;
(b = bottom, t = top, c = centre, l = left, r = right)

All other photographs, illustrations and diagrams by Peter Connolly.
Advisers: Dr Amanda Claridge, Oxford Institute of Archaelogy and Dr Joanne Berry, Oxford University.